George W. Bush

BY L. S. HASKELL

Published by The Child's World®
1980 Lookout Drive • Mankato, MN 56003-1705
800-599-READ • www.childsworld.com

Acknowledgments
The Child's World®: Mary Swensen, Publishing Director
Red Line Editorial: Editorial direction and production
The Design Lab: Design

Photographs ©: Pablo Martinez Monsivais/AP Images,
cover, 1; Doug Mills/AP Images, 4, 16; Hubert Boesl/
Picture-Alliance/DPA/AP Images, 7; Unimedia International/
Newscom, 8; Shutterstock Images, 11; Mark Elias/AP Image,
12; Ron Edmonds/AP Images, 15, 19; Julio Cortez/Houston
Chronicle/AP Images, 20

ISBN 9781503809086
LCCN 2016933845

Printed in the United States of America
Mankato, MN
June, 2016
PA02303

ABOUT THE AUTHOR

L. S. Haskell has written several
books for children on topics including
science, history, biography, and fiction.
She lives in Kentucky with her husband
and two children.

Table of Contents

The moment when George W. Bush heard about the September 11 attacks

CHAPTER ONE

A Brave Leader

It was early in September 2001. President
George W. Bush was traveling to Florida. As
president, he liked to visit classrooms. He liked to
meet teachers. He enjoyed listening to students read.
It was September 11, 2001. Bush visited Emma E.
Booker Elementary School. The school was in
Sarasota, Florida.

Bush went to a second grade class. The students
were excited to read. But their classroom was full of
strangers. **Journalists** were there. They had video
cameras and microphones. Security people were there.

They wanted to keep the president safe. Other guests were there, too. They wanted to meet the president.

While the students read, someone entered the classroom. His name was Andy Card. He worked for the president. He walked over to Bush. He leaned over and whispered in Bush's ear.

Later, the world would learn what Card whispered. He said, "America is under attack." Moments earlier, two airplanes had crashed. They flew into the World Trade Center buildings. They were in New York City.

Bush knew the journalists were taking pictures. He had to stay calm. He looked at the students. He thought about the children in America. He needed to keep them safe.

The students finished reading. Bush left the classroom. Americans wanted to hear from him.

The north tower of the World Trade Center collapsed at 10:28 a.m. on September 11, 2001.

They were worried. Bush understood that his words were important.

Bush spoke to the American people. He said, "**Terrorism** against our nation will not stand." This was an important moment for Bush. The country needed a brave leader. Bush showed strength and courage.

George W. Bush as a baby on his father's shoulders in 1947

CHAPTER TWO

The American Dream

George Walker Bush was born on July 6, 1946. He was born in New Haven, Connecticut. His parents were Barbara and George H. W. Bush. George was their oldest child. His family worked in the government. Prescott Bush was his grandfather. He was a U.S. **senator**. And George's father would one day be president.

George's family left Connecticut when he was young. They moved to Midland, Texas. George loved baseball, bicycles, and Cub Scouts.

George went to high school at Phillips Academy. It was in Andover, Massachusetts. It was a boarding school for boys. Students lived at school instead of at home.

Everything at the new school was different. Classes were hard. George missed his family and his friends.

Soon, George made new friends. He liked getting to know new people. His friendliness made him popular.

Phillips Academy taught George many important lessons. He learned that he could make friends anywhere. He found that he wasn't a quitter. He learned that he was a good leader.

George studied history in college. He went to Yale University. George joined the Air National Guard after college. He became a pilot.

George also concentrated on European and American studies at Yale.

George thought about growing up in Texas. He remembered watching football games on Friday nights. He remembered going to church on Sunday mornings. It was a safe town. This made him think about the American Dream.

George's idea of the American Dream was simple. It was a safe and happy world. He imagined camping, cookouts, and baseball games. George wanted everyone live their own American Dream.

Bush met many influential people during his father's campaign in 1988.

CHAPTER THREE

Road to the White House

★ ★ ★

Bush had many jobs as an adult. He worked in politics and baseball. He also worked in business. In 1988, his father ran for president. Bush moved to Washington, DC. He worked on his father's **campaign**.

In 1988, Bush's father became president. So Bush looked for a new job. In 1989, he bought a baseball team. A group of friends bought it with him. It was the Texas Rangers. Bush moved back to Texas.

In 1994, Bush ran for **governor** of Texas. He won. He was reelected four years later. Bush enjoyed being governor. He liked being a leader. He loved helping the people of Texas.

But Bush had bigger dreams in mind. He wanted to lead the country. He wanted to make Americans' lives better.

In 1999, Bush decided to run for president. The **election** was on November 7, 2000. Bush was the **candidate** for the Republican party. Al Gore was the candidate for the Democratic party. The election was close. Many votes had to be recounted.

The recounting took many weeks. Gore wanted to recount all of the votes. Bush did not. The Supreme Court listened to their argument. On December 12, the Court made a decision. The recount was over. Bush was the new president. He moved into the

Bush and Gore debated numerous times while running for president.

White House. Bush became the 43rd president of the United States.

Bush addressed the nation from the Oval Office after the September 11 attacks.

President of the United States

Bush still thought about the American Dream. He wanted children to have good schools. He also wanted to lower **taxes**.

Bush's plans changed on September 11, 2001. Four U.S. airplanes were **hijacked** that day. People crashed the planes on purpose. These people were not from the United States. Two planes hit the World Trade Center. Another plane flew into the Pentagon.

The last plane crashed in a field. Almost 3,000 Americans died in the attacks.

Bush promised to find the attackers. The government said it was al Qaeda. They are a terrorist group. The group hid in Afghanistan.

The United States went to war. **Troops** entered Afghanistan on October 7, 2001. Terrorists were also in Iraq. Bush wanted to enter Iraq, too. But some people thought this was wrong. They said Iraq did not hurt America. But Bush did not change his mind. The Iraq war started on March 19, 2003. The wars are now over. But there are still U.S. troops there today.

The United States was at war. But Bush didn't forget about the American Dream. He still wanted to make helpful laws.

Bush was surrounded by senators and children when he signed the No Child Left Behind Act in 2002.

Bush thought about schools. He wanted to make them better. He made a law for schools as governor of Texas. Texas schools had to give students tests. The tests were for reading and math. The tests showed when the students did better. Bush wanted to make the same law for the rest of the United States.

Bush at his book signing for *Decision Points* in 2010

He signed the law on January 8, 2002. It was called the No Child Left Behind Act.

Bush ran for reelection in 2004. He ran against John Kerry. Bush won.

Bush faced more problems. The wars continued. In 2005, a strong hurricane hit New Orleans, Louisiana. It was called Hurricane Katrina. It flooded parts of the South. The city was destroyed. More than 1,800 people died. Many people were mad at Bush. They thought he didn't help enough.

In 2008, the United States hit hard times. Many Americans lost their jobs. Others lost their homes. It took years for America to bounce back.

Bush served two terms as president. He moved back to Texas in 2009. Today he travels around the country. He gives speeches. He also likes to paint. In 2010, he wrote a book. It was called *Decision Points*.

Bush faced many problems as president. But he helped the country through hard times. He was a strong leader during September 11. He helped Americans feel safe again.

1940

← **July 6, 1946** George Walker Bush is born in New Haven, Connecticut.

← **1968** Bush graduates from Yale University.

← **1989** Bush buys the Texas Rangers baseball team.

← **1994** Bush is elected governor of Texas.

← **December 12, 2000** The Supreme Court holds that Bush won the 2000 presidential election.

← **September 11, 2001** The World Trade Center is attacked.

← **October 7, 2001** The war in Afghanistan begins.

← **January 8, 2002** Bush signs the No Child Left Behind Act.

← **March 19, 2003** The war in Iraq begins.

← **November 2, 2004** Bush is reelected president of the United States.

← **August 29, 2005** Hurricane Katrina hits the Gulf Coast.

← **October 2008** America falls on hard times.

← **November 9, 2010** Bush's book, *Decision Points*, is published.

2015

campaign (kam-PAYN) When people try to win an election, they organize their activities in a campaign. Bush gave speeches during his campaign to become president.

candidate (KAN-di-dayt) A candidate is a person who runs for office. Bush was the presidential candidate in 2000.

election (i-LEK-shun) An election is when people choose a leader by voting. In the election of 2000, Bush was chosen as the president.

governor (GUV-uh-ner) A governor is the head of a state or colony. Bush was the governor of Texas.

hijacked (HY-jakt) When something is hijacked, it is taken by force. Terrorists hijacked four airplanes on September 11, 2001.

journalists (JUR-nuh-lists) Journalists are news writers. The journalists wrote news stories about Bush's visit to Emma E. Booker Elementary School.

senator (SEN-uh-ter) A person who joins the Senate, one of the governing bodies of the United States, is a senator. Bush's grandfather served as a U.S. senator.

taxes (TAKS-is) Taxes are money that people and companies pay to the government. Bush wanted to lower taxes for Americans.

terrorism (TER-uh-riz-uhm) Terrorism is when people scare others into obedience by using violence. The attacks on September 11 were acts of terrorism.

troops (TROOPZ) Troops are a group of soldiers. In 2001, troops entered Afghanistan.

In the Library

Benoit, Peter. *September 11 Then and Now*. New York: Scholastic, 2011.

Burgan, Michael. *George W. Bush*. Mankato, MN: Child's World, 2009.

Hajeski, Nancy J. *The Big Book of Presidents: From George Washington to Barack Obama*. New York: Sky Pony Press, 2015.

On the Web

Visit our Web site for links about
George W. Bush: **childsworld.com/links**

Note to Parents, Teachers, and Librarians: We routinely verify our Web links to make sure they are safe and active sites. So encourage your readers to check them out!

INDEX